WACKY COMPARISONS

HOW LONG?

WACKY WAYS TO COMPARE LENGTH

by Jessica Gunderson

illustrated by Igor Sinkovec

How long is a **SHIP**? Or a **SNAKE** that slithers?

Is either as long as the **MISSISSIPPI RIVER**?

A **SHARK'S TOOTH**, a **DINO** long gone— look inside to see **HOW LONG!**

PICTURE WINDOW BOOKS

a capstone imprint

Listen up, elephant,
no ifs, ands, or buts,

your **TRUNK** is as long as
42 PEANUTS.

1 FOOTBALL FIELD is just as long as **960** SANDWICHES joined in song.

4

1 field = 360 ft. (110 m); 1 sandwich = 4½ in. (11 cm)

3 POINTY HUMAN TEETH, it's the truth,

are nearly the length of

1 GREAT WHITE SHARK TOOTH.

How long was APATOSAURUS, head to tail?

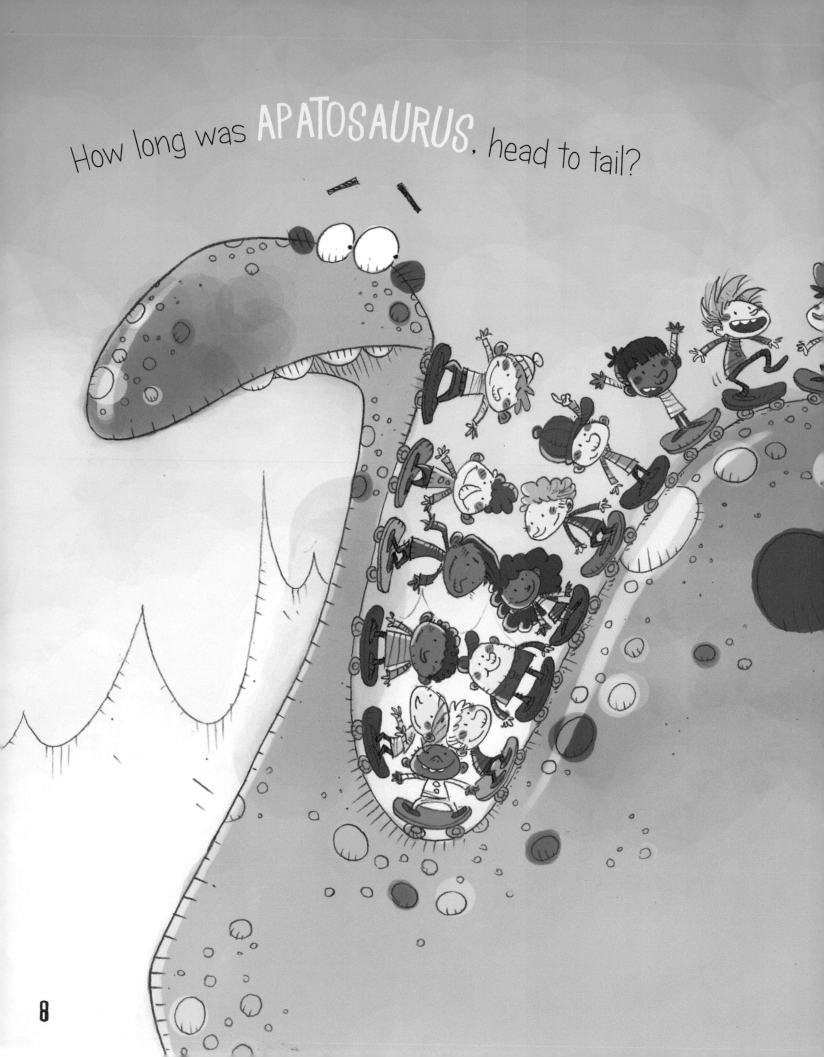

Along its back **30** SKATEBOARDERS sail.

1 apatosaurus = 74 ft. (23 m); 1 skateboard = 2½ ft. (76 cm)

7 STICKS OF LICORICE stuck together

equal the length of

1 PEACOCK FEATHER.

1 feather = 5 ft. (1.5 m); 1 licorice stick = 8 in. (20 cm)

A ROCKET TO THE MOON is a

3-DAY RIDE.

How long for a

CAR DRIVING 65?

153 DAYS

(at 65 miles [105 kilometers] per hour)

distance to the moon = 238,855 miles (384,400 km)
rocket speed = 6,635 miles (10,678 km) per hour

How many **RATS** does it take to make

1 snake = 20 ft. (6.1 m); 1 rat = 1½ ft. (46 cm)

1 ROYAL CRUISE SHIP stretches out to sea.

16

It's the length of
170 MATTRESSES
fit for a queen.

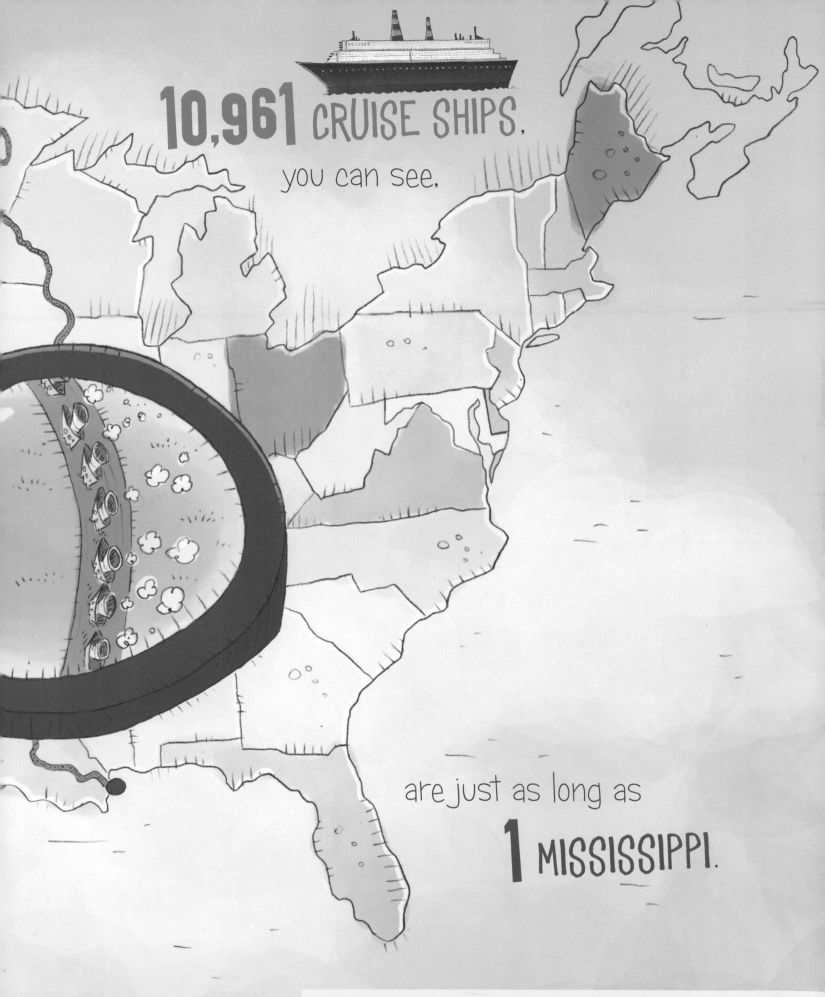

10,961 CRUISE SHIPS, you can see, are just as long as **1** MISSISSIPPI.

1 river = 2,350 miles (3,782 km); 1 ship = 1,132 ft. (345 m)

An **EAGLE** spreads its wings so wide—

the length of **13** **DOLLAR BILLS** side by side.

1 eagle = 6 ft., 10 in. (2.1 m); 1 bill = 6¹/₈ in. (16 cm)